BIRDS OF THE SEA, SHORE AND TUNDRA

BIRDS OF THE SEA, SHORE AND TUNDRA

THEODORE CROSS

WEIDENFELD & NICOLSON
New York

PUBLISHED BY WEIDENFELD & NICOLSON, NEW YORK
A DIVISION OF WHEATLAND CORPORATION
841 BROADWAY
NEW YORK, NEW YORK 10003-4793

INTERNATIONAL STANDARD BOOK NUMBER 1-55584-385-9
LIBRARY OF CONGRESS CATALOG CARD NUMBER 88-092284

COLOR SEPARATIONS BY ESSEX COLOUR, ESSEX, ENGLAND
PRINTED IN ITALY BY AMILCARE PIZZI, S.P.A.

THIS BOOK IS PRINTED ON ACID-FREE PAPER.

DESIGNED BY MIKE ROSE

FIRST EDITION

10 9 8 7 6 5 4 3 2 1

Dedicated to
RALPH W. SCHREIBER, PH.D.
1942–1988

INTRODUCTION

My passion for photographing birds came late in life. I was fifty years old before I first pointed a camera in the direction of a bird. Since then, the thousands of hours I have spent with birds have been ones of indescribable pleasure. Today, the memories of expeditions to the High Arctic and the Central Pacific evoke the same feelings of nostalgia as do my childhood memories of moonlit porches and secret hiding places. Each spring, over the past fourteen years, I have thrilled to the anticipation of returning to my secret island of colonial nesting waterbirds in southern New Jersey. Next spring I will make my fourth trip to the Texas Gulf Coast, searching once more for a missing colony of the most exciting bird in the United States, the reddish egret. Then there are the memories of those rare days of spectacular good fortune when, for some inexplicable reason, the light is right and the birds you are watching do all the wondrous things you always prayed they would do. When this happens you genuinely feel that God has his hand on your camera. When I was younger I struggled to find answers to some of the most vexing social problems of our time. Now, at age 64, I sometimes think I would rather take a truly great photograph of a red-tailed tropicbird than find the truth about the higher meaning of life.

In recent years, at least, the pleasures of bird photography are closely connected with the process of growing older. Photographing birds, along with my family and work, have combined to give me—in the words of Erik Erikson—an emotionally successful life in which the inevitable despair that comes with physical deterioration of the body is defeated by a sense of personal wholeness. Whether one's career is law, business, publishing or hauling up the flag of revolution, watching, studying and photographing birds are superb ways of keeping one's mind off one's own mortality and staying very much alive. For the rest of you I hope you will discover something like this before it's too late.

I would like to thank the scores of friends who have helped this book come about. They are: Eleanor Alefounder, Gerald Atkins, Susan Bailey, Dave Ballay, Andrew Barty-King, David Blankinship, Gary Blizzard, Tomas Blohm, Alexander Reid Brash, Tom and Virginia Brown, Bud and Sadie Buller, G. Vernon Byrd, Clint Campbell, Al Chartier, Nancy Claflin, Mary Cross, Dan Dennett, Randy Deshotel, Rick Draper, Roger Drummond, Darrel Dupont, Allan Ensminger, Michelle Iuviene Epstein, Richard Ffrench, William J. (Friday) Fluman, Dick Folta, Dick Fontenot, Peter Frederick, Granger Frost, Frank Gonzales, Mary Lou Goodwin, Jesse Grantham, Bill Harrison, Bill Herrington, Mike Hoke, Jan and Denise Hoogesteger, Ted Joanen, Villi and Lola Jonasson, Dr. M. Philip Kahl, Bruno Kern, Robert Kimble, Joe Kowal, Rodney Krey, Elaine Kursch, Keith Landry, Carl Lane, Jim Lane, Perry Langston, Patrick Lawrence, Rochelle Lewis, Steve Littleton, Charles Luthin, Stewart MacDonald, James Massey, Jr., Sharon L. Milder, Gus Miller, Jay Mills, Billy Morris, Jim Mott, David Nettleship, Paul Neuthaler, Liz Noseworthy, Prof. James Parnell, Richard Paul, Roger and Shirley Perry, John Piatt, Liz Pilling, Dr. Robert Pyle, Paul Ratson, David Richard, Prof. Gilberto Rios, Harriet Ripinsky, Dr. William Robertson, Dr. James A. Rodgers, Mike Rose, Jack Sacher, Peter Savoie, Joann Scanlon, Dr. Ralph and Betty Anne Schreiber, Tom Sharp, J.C. Shaver, Gregg Silstorf, Michael Smith, Gene Snow, Bea Spradlir, Jack Svedberg, Johnny Swanner, David Tidbury, Rebecca Tracy, George Trafford, Claude Tremblay, Real Tremblay, Randy Tripp, Roger Vincent, Jr., Dr. Reed Wardens, Ray Whatley, Mike Wilcox, and Dewey Wills.

THEODORE CROSS

Princeton, New Jersey
August, 1988

THE BIRDS

CATTLE EGRET This egret is an African import that has undergone a huge range expansion in the United States. Ordinarily the dullest of the herons, this pair appears in its nuptial splendor of brilliant red, orange and buff.

CATTLE EGRET

above. CATTLE EGRET

right. SNOWY EGRET Widespread throughout the Americas and the most beautiful of the herons, the breeding snowy egret, develops transluscent white plumes that cascade down the back and recurve back toward the head. In feeding, it dashes around in shallow pools much like the reddish egret, with lots of foot scraping to stir up action, but with less parasoling of the wings.

above. SNOWY EGRET

right. AMERICAN EGRET Except for the rare great
white heron of Florida, the American egret is the
largest and most aristocratic of our herons. With
splendid four-foot nuptial plumes, it stands three
feet tall with a wingspread of four and a half feet.

AMERICAN EGRET

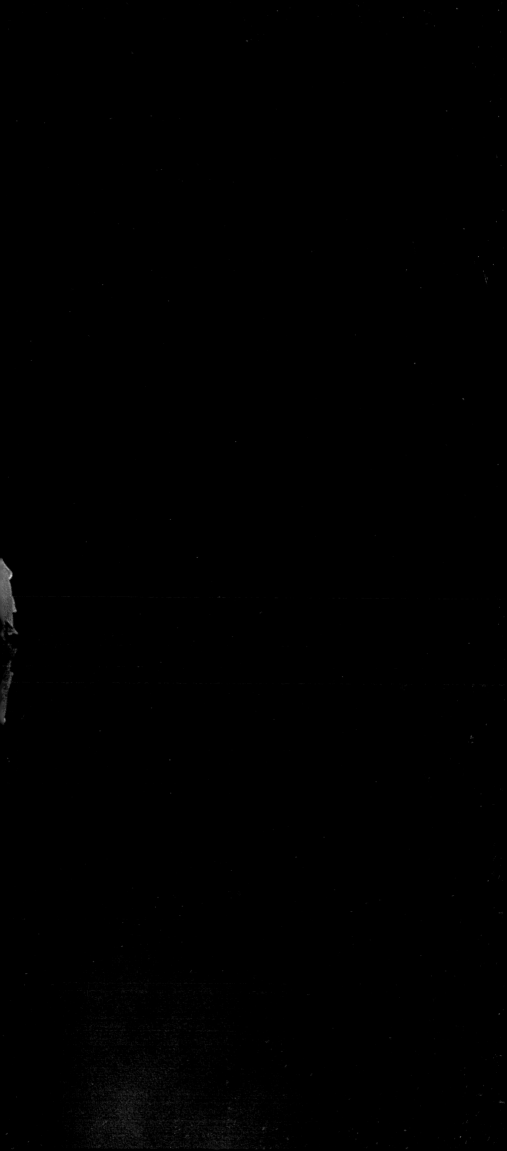

AMERICAN EGRET *and overleaf.*

REDDISH EGRET The reddish egret, wrote
ornithologist Arthur Cleveland Bent, "fairly
bristles with plumes that stand out like the quills
of a porcupine, giving the bird quite a formidable
appearance, terrifying to its enemies."

left and overleaf. REDDISH EGRET
White phase

REDDISH EGRET

above. TRICOLORED HERON The tricolored heron, more often known as the Louisiana heron, is the most common heron of the Gulf states. In nuptial phase it is unmatched in color and beauty, often acquiring a bright blue bill, orange legs and ornamental plumes of blue and chestnut.

right and overleaf. GREAT BLUE HERON This majestic wading bird is found throughout the continental United States. Shy and vigilant, the great blue is almost impossible to approach.

LEAST BITTERN The smallest of the herons, the least bittern is a shy and solitary hermit of the marsh. When a stranger passes, she assumes her straight-up defense posture with bill pointed to the sky—and becomes indistinguishable from the surrounding reeds and cattails.

left GREEN HERON The green heron is not green but rather rust, or chestnut, and blue. Silent, still and hunkered down next to a mangrove pool, she customarily waits for food to come her way. In the nesting season, the legs of the male are a striking orange. In advanced stages of incubation, this pair has lost some of its nuptial coloring.

GREEN HERON

left and above. LITTLE BLUE HERON The unusual
feature of the little blue heron is that for most of
its first year of life it is white and easily confused
with the snowy egret or reddish egret in white
phase. Here a mature little blue heron is shown
late in the breeding cycle when the bright marine
blue behind the eyes is turning grayish blue.

above and right. LITTLE BLUE HERON

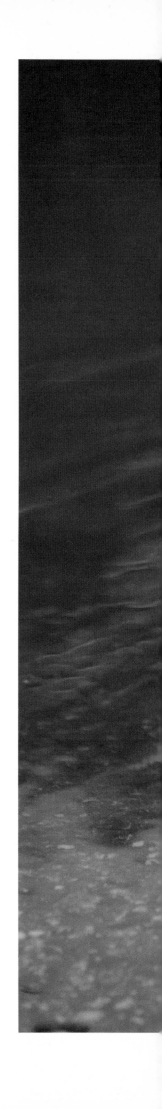

above and right. YELLOW-CROWNED NIGHT HERON
The unflappable though solitary yellow-crowned
night heron will nest within a few feet of parking
lots or office buildings. She has a huge breeding
range extending from the northeastern United
States through southern Brazil, Peru and the
Galapagos Islands.

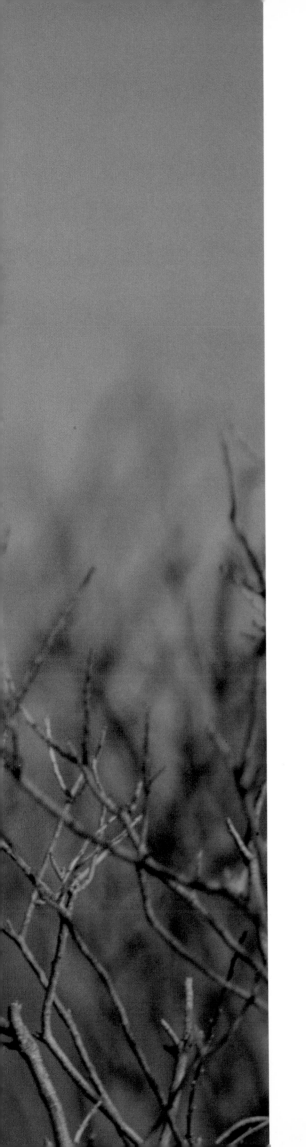

BLACK-CROWNED NIGHT HERON Probably the most common heron in the world, the stocky black-crowned night heron commonly dozes all day, heading at sunset for its feeding ground.

WHITE IBIS With breathtaking snow-white plumage, and in breeding season showing brilliant red beak and legs, the white ibis nests in large colonies in the mangrove islands of the Gulf states. Unlike the herons that target individual prey, it uses its downward curved beak to probe randomly for crayfish and other food.

left and above. WHITE IBIS

above. WHITE IBIS

right. SCARLET IBIS The most brilliant of all the
ibises, the scarlet ibis is found only in South
America, where it is seen in Trinidad and breeds
in huge colonies particularly in the western
savannas of Venezuela.

WHITE-FACED IBIS Like the cattle egret, this Old World species appears to have crossed the Atlantic and settled in the United States. Considered sacred by the ancient Egyptians, this bird and its glossy brown cousin finds protection in the drab colors of their plumage. It is distinguishable from the glossy ibis during the breeding season, when it develops a patch of white feathers around its eyes.

YELLOW-BILLED STORK This African stork is found breeding in colonies in East Africa and in the Okavanga Delta of Botswana.

WOOD STORK Possibly the world's homeliest bird,
the wood stork is the only native American
stork. On a hot day it is commonly seen soaring
over the big cypress swamps of Florida,
mounting in circles to tremendous heights.

above and right. ROSEATE SPOONBILL A spectacular
though grotesque wader that feeds for small fish
and crustaceans by sweeping its broad, flattened
bill from side to side as it slowly marches
through the mangrove pools of coastal Florida,
Louisiana and Texas.

SPOONBILL CHICKS Still feeding on shrimp and crustaceans regurgitated by their parents, the bills of these nestlings are not yet formed in the familiar shape of the spoonbill spatula.

RED-TAILED TROPICBIRD Brilliant white with coral red bill and long red tail streamers, the red-tailed tropicbird is probably the world's most beautiful seabird. They are strong and graceful fliers, but, like the albatross, the tropicbird is a disaster on land. Its short legs are so far back on its body that it has to roll and shove itself forward like a person without arms or legs.

RED-TAILED TROPICBIRD The red-tailed tropicbird approaches the nest site by hovering over the scaevola bush that protects the eggs and then plunging through the leaves and branches to its nest on the ground.

left and above. RED-TAILED TROPICBIRD The red-tailed tropicbird nests on remote tropical islands of the Pacific. Large numbers are found on Christmas and Midway Islands. They never come to land except to breed. During the summer months, tropicbirds leave their nests at midday and perform high-altitude acrobatic dances, often fluttering backwards—all accompanied by raucous cries and screaming.

left and overleaf. LAYSAN ALBATROSS Upwards of 100,000 Laysan albatross breed on the tiny Pacific Navy atoll of Midway. During the long nesting season, neither smoke, noise, Japanese bombs nor the eviction procedures of the U.S. Navy have been sufficient to dislodge these ocean wanderers.

above and opposite. LAYSAN ALBATROSS

above and overleaf. BLACK-FOOTED ALBATROSS This is the albatross that is most familiar to mariners. Effortlessly soaring on ocean thermals, it follows ships for days at a time. Large colonies of black-foots breed on Midway and in the western Hawaiian Islands.

left. LAYSAN ALBATROSS

above, right and overleaf. RED-FOOTED BOOBY
A frequent follower of ships, the red-footed
booby is the only member of its species that is
at home in the branches of a tree. It ranges
worldwide in tropical oceans and breeds in large
numbers on Fanning, Christmas and Palmyra
Islands in the Pacific Ocean south of Hawaii.

BROWN BOOBY Found on the equatorial islands of the Pacific, the ground-nesting brown booby has no need to engage in hokey, broken-wing defenses. Approach too near the nest and its double-hinged and vise-like beak may impress a permanent lock on your hand. Courtship display is the traditional bowing, strutting, stretching, bill clacking and sky pointing.

left and above. FRIGATE BIRD When this lugubrious fellow is ready to breed, he sits on a bush and lures in a female by inflating his scarlet throat pouch, clattering his bill and flashing the white underside of his wings.

Frigate birds and red-footed boobies roosting at sunset on the Pacific atoll of Christmas Island.

MASKED BOOBY Unlike the pelican, which gets her food near the surface, a booby plunges into the ocean from spectacular heights and actually pursues fish six or seven feet under water. The masked booby ranges around the world in tropical and subtropical waters.

above. MASKED BOOBY

right. SOOTY TERN The sooty tern is the most abundant equatorial seabird. Sooties nest on Christmas Island in the Pacific in colonies of one million birds or more. Since it comes ashore only during the breeding season and can't rest on the water, ornithologists conclude that the adult bird flies continually for seven months of the year without touching ground and the immature bird is steadily in the air for the first *five years* of its life.

left and above. CASPIAN TERN Our largest tern is the size of a herring gull. It commonly nests at the fringes of large colonies of royal and sandwich terns and preys on their nests and nestlings.

above and right. LITTLE TERN Beset by the four-wheel beach-driving craze, this delicate white bird with a black cap and a forked tail is seriously threatened in the United States. She lays her eggs in nothing more than a shallow scrape in the sand. Her nest protection is limited to highly efficient dive bombing at unwanted intruders.

BROWN NODDY The brown noddy tern nests aboveground on a bed of sticks in a bush or low tree on the equatorial islands of the Pacific Ocean. Like its breeding companion, the sooty tern, the noddy breeds year-round and disappears when nesting season is finished.

above and right. FAIRY TERN The so-called love
tern is the only bird that leads much of its life
balanced on a tightrope. Without building a nest,
this delicate snow-white tern lays and guards a
single egg on a branch or in the crotch of a tree.
A curious bird that hovers about humans, the
fairy tern breeds in large numbers on Midway,
Christmas and other tropical islands.

left and above. ARCTIC TERN The fabulous Arctic tern holds all records in migratory flight. It summers in the Arctic and winters in the Antarctic, making two 12,000-mile trips a year. Its blood-red bill, short legs and unexpectedly large tail and long wings are its distinguishing marks.

right and overleaf. BLACK SKIMMER Like sandpipers and spoonbills, the black skimmer plays the odds. Instead of targeting its food, it glides just inches above the water with its extra-long lower mandible audibly slicing the surface of the water. When the scarlet beak touches something edible, an automatic reflex snaps the jaws shut.

HEERMANN'S GULL Tens of thousands of these gray-bellied gulls gather to breed in the spring on the Island of Raza off the coast of Mexico in Baja, California.

above and right. HEERMANN'S GULL

HEERMANN'S GULL Like most other birds, copulation among the Heermann's gull is difficult because the male has no penis. Mating, which has been compared to docking two Apollo spacecraft, requires the exquisitely perfect touching of two openings called "cloaca" while the male flaps his wings for balance.

preceding pages. BONAPARTE'S GULL The Bonaparte's gull is named after Charles Lucien Bonaparte, a distinguished French zoologist and nephew of Emperor Napoleon. It is a handsome, black-hooded and tern-like gull that nests in trees. Pay a visit to their breeding grounds in the coniferous forests of the Canadian subarctic and wildly screaming adults will persistently dive at your head.

SWALLOW-TAILED GULL The swallow-tailed gull is the only nocturnal gull, which explains the large light-gathering eyes. The bird is local in the Galapagos.

ATLANTIC PUFFIN The Atlantic puffin is a small auk with a brilliant red, blue and yellow beak. It nests in rocky underground burrows on island cliffs in Greenland, Iceland and the Canadian Arctic.

left, above, first overleaf and second overleaf. GANNET
Large and graceful seabirds with six-foot
wingspans, gannets breed in huge colonies on
remote island cliffs of the North Atlantic. Sky
pointing, head wagging, neck rubbing and beak
rattling are part of the mating ritual.

left and preceding pages.
WHITE PELICAN Save for the nearly extinct California condor, this magnificent white bird with orange bill has the largest wingspan of any flying bird in North America. Unlike its smaller cousin the brown pelican, it never dives for fish but often engages in cooperative hunting in which a group of swimming birds surround a school of fish, scooping up their victims with their pouches as they draw the circle tighter.

above. BROWN PELICAN Eating one-fifth of its body weight every day, the brown pelican spots its prey, plunges downward into the water from thirty feet, survives a crash that no airplane could endure, and traps the fish in its gular pouch.

left and overleaf. AMERICAN OYSTERCATCHER This chunky black and white shorebird with yellow eyes and orange beak is named for its ability to use its hard bill to penetrate the shell and snip the adductor muscles of oysters, mussels and clams. Its principal failing is its habit of laying its eggs unprotected on the open beach or at the edge of a parking lot.

WILLET The willet is a large, dull and inelegant shorebird until it flies and displays its flashing white tail and black-and-white wings. It breeds on the Atlantic coast from New Jersey to Florida. When a predator arrives, nesting territories are disregarded and all willets in the area will mob the intruder.

ARCTIC LOON The Arctic loon nests at the edge of tundra lakes across the Canadian Arctic from Alaska to Hudson Bay. At the first sign of danger, she slides on her belly down a short, slippery runway to the water. To the Cree Indians, the eerie call of the loon was the scream of a brave who was denied entrance to heaven. Writer John McPhee has likened the tremolo of the loon to the ''laugh of the deeply insane.''

left and above. BLACK-NECKED STILT The black-
necked stilt is a graceful shorebird with comically
long red legs. Though a poor nest planner, she
is a superb engineer. When the floodwaters
arrive—as they always do—the stilt simply
gathers more material and elevates its nest
that was built too close to the shore.

GODWIT CHICK Twenty-four hours after kicking themselves free of their shells, these little feather balls catch their own insects and swim across good-sized tundra lakes. Ten weeks after hatching, they set forth on their fall migration from their Arctic breeding grounds to southern Argentina and Chile.

HUDSONIAN GODWIT On its way to early extinction
in the 1940s, the Hudsonian godwit is now a
common breeder in the Canadian subarctic.
In the fall migration, huge flocks gather in late
August in James Bay from where they fly 2,800
miles nonstop to the delta of the Orinoco River,
the first stop on the way to their Patagonian
wintering grounds.

WHIMBREL The whimbrel or Hudsonian curlew, declared almost extinct in 1930, now nests in large numbers on the shores of Hudson Bay. If this subtly colored wader with a downcurved beak had a white rump, it would be a Eurasian curlew whose appearance in 1978 on Martha's Vineyard set the bird world on its head.

COMMON SNIPE A sandpiper of the bogs
and marshes, known for its hollow tremolo
''winnowing'' produced by the vibrating
tail feathers of the diving bird.

left and above. RED KNOT A spectacular long-distance traveler, the red knot breeds above the magnetic North Pole. After several days of trekking, this one was found near Eureka on Ellesmere Island. In late summer this stocky, cinnamon-colored sandpiper moves into its coastal staging areas and then migrates in huge flocks to South America where it winters along the southern coast of Argentina.

RED PHALAROPE The male phalarope incubates the eggs and assumes all family care until the chicks are self-sufficient. The female pictured here in breeding plumage is more brightly colored than the male. After laying, she is known to run off with another suitor and start a new family.

left RED PHALAROPE

above. BAIRD'S SANDPIPER Baird's
sandpiper is one of the small look-alike
sandpipers known as ''peeps.'' She nests
on the tundra of the high Canadian Arctic
as far north as Axel Heiberg and Ellesmere Islands.
This one was sitting near the village of Cambridge
Bay on Victoria Island in the Canadian
Northwest Territories.

left. RED-BREASTED MERGANSER This rakish and
somewhat comical diving duck has a streamlined
body and saw-toothed bill ideally suited for
pursuing fish under water.

above. ROSS'S GULL The Ross's gull is a rare and
beautiful rosy-hued gull of the high Arctic.
The only known breeding sites are in northeastern
Siberia. Recently a single pair has appeared each
year, nesting near the tundra pools of Churchill,
Manitoba.

PIPING PLOVER The piping plover is a sparrow-sized shorebird with feathers the color of dry beach sand. Now seriously threatened, she lays four khaki-colored eggs in shell-adorned scrapes or on sparsely vegetated beaches. She currently spends much of her time in feigned injury displays and ''escort'' behavior designed to lead intruders away from her nest.

SEMIPALMATED PLOVER This little shorebird that breeds on the subarctic tundra is a master of the wounded bird act. Approach the nest—a mere depression in a sandy or gravelly beach—and the parent flutters its wings, falls on its side and drags its fanned-out tail on the ground for fifty yards from its eggs.

above and right. GOLDEN PLOVER Nesting
among miniature Arctic rhododendron and
lichen-covered rocks, the golden plover's eggs
are perfectly camouflaged. She is an intrepid
traveler and a marvelous flier, making two annual
7,000-mile trips from the Canadian subarctic to
the southern tip of Patagonia. The soft, sweet,
mournful piping of the golden plover is often the
first thrilling and nostalgic call to greet the bird
watcher returning in the spring to the Arctic
tundra.

KILLDEER An elegant plover with chestnut wings and two black stripes over her white breast, the killdeer is the undisputed champion of false brooding (settling on nonexistent eggs) and fake injury to draw intruders away from her nest. This inland breeder is known to farmers throughout North America. Her vast breeding range extends from southern Canada to northern Chile.

HARRIS'S SPARROW Audubon named this sparrow with the handsome plumage after Edward Harris, a companion on his 1843 Missouri River expedition. It nests in the wet hummocks of the subarctic tundra.

SANDERLINGS These are the tireless little sandpipers seen on the beach running ahead of waves like windup toys. Among the great wanderers, these little puffs of feathers migrate each year from central Chile to their nesting grounds in northeastern Greenland. In wintertime the sanderling exchanges its rusty plumage for pale gray.

above. DUNLIN Gathering in immense numbers during the spring and fall migrations, dunlins feed nonstop on sand and mud flats. They are famous for aerial maneuvers with flocks of thousands flying in dense clouds, making perfectly synchronized turns. Once the most common shorebird of North America, the breeding population appears to have crashed in recent years.

left. SHORT-BILLED DOWITCHER Standing belly deep in tundra pools of the lower Canadian Arctic, these chunky snipe-like waders feed like a sewing machine. The short, stocky wings permit instant flight. Like most shorebirds, the precocious chicks are taking short flights by the time they are two weeks old.

AMERICAN AVOCET Standing tall on elegant blue legs, the avocet marches through shallow ponds in the western United States, feeding by swinging her upturned beak from side to side like a farmer swinging a scythe.

LONG-BILLED CURLEW The largest member of the curlew family has never recovered from the hunting decimation of two generations ago. The remnants of huge flocks that resided in all the eastern states are now known only to the farmers, ranchers and sheepmen of Montana, Utah and a few other western states.

left. HUDSONIAN GODWIT Hudsonian godwit protesting an intruder in her spruce woods nesting territory. Calling frantically, she gracefully glides to a treetop, raises her wings straight up for a split second and then folds them deliberately.

above. STILT SANDPIPER Courage is the fundamental trait of nesting shorebirds. Here a stilt sandpiper has the impertinence to hold on its nest while a gigantic creature a thousand times its height takes a picture at a distance of ten feet. The stilt sandpiper commonly associates with yellowlegs and dowitchers with which it is often confused.

LESSER YELLOWLEGS The yellowlegs is the Paul Revere of the bird community. Whenever there is a disturbance in her spruce woods nesting territory, she flies to a perch on a tall conifer and screams bloody murder. The yellowlegs is another of those fabulous long-distance travelers, flying each year from as far south as Tierra del Fuego to its muskeg nesting territories on Hudson Bay, Canada.

above and opposite. WHISTLING SWAN The most abundant of the North American swans, the whistling swan nests in the Canadian Arctic. One of the great ornithological spectacles of North America occurs in the fall when tens of thousands of them arrive at their wintering grounds in the estuaries of Chesapeake Bay.

left and above. WHISTLING SWAN

left. BLACK SWAN Concentrations of 2,000 to
5,000 black swans are common on many lakes
in Australia and Tasmania. Flying over the Great
Dividing Range in New South Wales, they often
reach an altitude of 8,000 feet.

above. MANDARIN DUCK With fabulously
irridescent colors on the crown and the side,
the mandarin duck of the Far East is now
well-established in Scotland.

above and opposite. SNOW GOOSE Snow geese, the most abundant of all geese, breed in huge colonies on the Arctic shores of Alaska and Canada. In the early fall migration, up to 35,000 birds rest and feed for about eight weeks at New Jersey's Brigantine Wildlife Refuge.

right and overleaf. SNOWY OWL Breeding in the icy wastes of the high Arctic tundra, the snowy owl is dependent wholly on the lemming population for food. The typical snowy owl nest consists of a huge oversupply of lemming carcasses provided by the anxious male to his brooding mate. In years when the lemming population crashes, snowy owls may be seen as far south as the northern United States. The round head and absence of ear tufts suggest a cat rather than a bird.

above and right. OSPREY A fierce looking bird of prey with a wingspan up to six feet, the osprey is found almost worldwide. A fine sportsman that prefers live fish, the osprey plunges precipitously from as high as 300 feet, disappears into the water in a cloud of spray, and slowly rises with its ice-hook-like grip on a fish which it then carries like a torpedo to its nest. The osprey nests for life and returns to the same nest year after year.

right and overleaf. MERLIN Formerly known as the pigeon hawk, this small falcon summers near the northern tree line of North America. In the breeding season, this fearless bundle of energy consumes 400 or 500 small birds, usually sparrows, warblers, sandpipers and plovers.

ANHINGA This evil-looking bird with a snake's neck, dagger bill and cold red eyes is a peerless spearfisher. In the drying-out position, the silver-white forewings look like the ivory keys on a piano.

NOTE ON TECHNIQUE

Bird photography is not an accepted academic discipline. There is, for example, no body of knowledge on photographing birds. But people still ask what it is that I have learned. In large measure bird photography is an exercise in strategic thinking. Most good pictures come from hard thought about the image you want to have and then plotting alternative ways of getting that picture. For example, when you arrive in an unknown place—typically a new island or bird colony—it is important to scout the situation. Walk around for an hour or more with binoculars but without your camera. Birds always do repetitive things. See what is where; see where it goes; see what keeps coming back to the same place. Birds always have a favorite place to sit or display. Find out what it is that brings them back. Yes, it is pleasant to sit and wonder about the meaning of the call of the curlew. But for the bird photographer it is more important to find out what she is about to do when she calls.

By the time you have come to map and understand this new island or situation, the light may be getting bad. Now is the time to think about the plan for the next day. Ask yourself what pictures you want and how to get them, where you want to be for an east wind and morning light or a west wind and late afternoon light. In seeking the picture you want, follow your whims, try things out, play with various alternatives. Repeatedly, ask yourself hypothetical questions. If I take up this position or that position, what am I likely to get?

I feel then that the process of successful photography of birds in action is essentially experimental. But there are some rules that make for better pictures. Work with early morning or late afternoon light. Unless you can contrive to be on a twelve-foot ladder looking down, pictures taken between 10 A.M. and 3 P.M. are usually a waste of film. Try to catch peak action, include the natural habitat, and avoid putting the bird in the center of the picture. Shun the perfectly framed and focused "tunnel" shots taken through a long lens. Usually they are boring or trite unless the subject is very unusual or rare. Learn to stay put and wait for the great moment when light, action and luck combine to give you an exciting picture. Don't even think of pursuing the photography of birds if you're the kind of person who has to ask if it is time for lunch. Resist electronic light, always bracket exposures, and use Kodachrome 64 or 25 film. In my view, it's still too early to trust Kodachrome 200.

Don't be afraid to try your luck. The camera is intolerant of those who break the rules, but somehow it is forgiving of those who photograph birds.

T L C

Publisher THEODORE CROSS is the author of *Black Capitalism* (Atheneum 1969) and, with his wife, Mary Cross, *Behind the Great Wall, a Photographic Essay on China* (Atheneum 1979). His most recent book is *The Black Power Imperative* (Faulkner Books 1984). He is a foremost spokesman for black economic development and in 1970 designed the Washington-based Opportunity Funding Corporation at the request of the White House.

The author has lectured on minority economics and law at Harvard, Cornell and the University of Virginia. For many years he was a Trustee of Amherst College and Chairman of the Investment Committee of its Board of Trustees. The author is a Trustee of the Folger Shakespeare Library in Washington and is a past Public Governor of the American Stock Exchange. He is a graduate of Harvard Law School, where he was an editor of the *Harvard Law Review*.

MATTIA BONETTI

FOREWORD BY ADRIAN DANNATT

ESSAYS BY JACQUES GRANGE, MARIE-LAURE JOUSSET,

REED KRAKOFF, AND PRINCESS GLORIA VON THURN UND TAXIS

FEATURING PHOTOGRAPHY BY REED KRAKOFF

PAUL KASMIN GALLERY

3 DROPS TABLE
Lacquered wood and clear acrylic
75 x 150 x 150 cm
29½ x 59 x 59 in
Édition La Galerie Italienne
Paris, 2008

MR. JEAN-PIERRE LEHMANN AND MRS. RACHEL LEHMANN RESIDENCE

Bench and side tables: lacquered
hand-sculpted wood and leather
Headboard: wood structure upholstered
with Boussac fabric and metallic leather
Bedspread: Boussac fabric with
varnished leather appliqué
East Hampton, New York, 2004

he life and work of Mattia Bonetti stands as testament to the vast creative potential of ambiguity, uncertainty, paradox, and duality—and an absolute refusal to be one thing when it is possible to embody a multitude of possibilities simultaneously. His work exemplifies a certain strand of postmodernism that is both practical and theoretical; it embodies a philosophy of instability and witty subterfuge—a celebration of the principle of both/and rather than either/or and the quality in which everything, even identity, stays fluid. The combination of this philosophy and a dedication to the highest and most traditional standards of French classical workmanship, found within the ateliers of artisans and trained apprentices, results in an oeuvre whose inspiration (and perhaps insolence) is matched by its formal integrity. This ambiguity might even be traced through Bonetti's own biography, from his homeland of the Ticino region, which incorporates the bravura exuberance of Italy and the rigor and integrity of Swiss culture, to a childhood in the sixties, surrounded by both the authenticity of traditional antiques and the radical experiments of the era. But apart from such weary design tropes as "zeitgeist" and "upbringing," what Bonetti ultimately embodies is the sheer visceral pleasure of the artist, the creative imagination let loose, regardless of whether the results are to be hung upon a wall or tethered to domestic use.

Adrian Dannatt

5

Adrian Dannatt: You are very much the artist, in that all of your ideas come from the initial drawings you create.

Mattia Bonetti: If I start doodling, as I always do when I'm on the telephone, there is always a risk that, however fantastical it might look, I am going to have to end up making the sketch into actual three-dimensional furniture!

AD: The process seems very direct: You create a freehand sketch, which is turned into a series of very detailed technical drawings, and then these are given to the artisan craftsmen you work with in Paris.

MB: There is usually a sort of logic: a progression, a line. This is often directed by the materials I work with and am currently fascinated by, and even by associations and shapes. But sometimes the work comes out abruptly, as with the Abyss table: It came out like that from the first sketch. I knew it needed to be sculpted first as a scale model, as it was too complicated a shape; it couldn't go from paper straight to an artisan to realize. There are often pieces like that table, which need that intermediary stage. This helps me control the shape from A to Z. At every stage I am present, and very demanding.

AD: Do you feel that the furniture created from your own imagination must be completed exactly as first drawn, even when you've made it hard for yourself to do so? Do you have to "obey" the drawing you've done or can you abandon it if it's too difficult?

MB: I try to stay with what I first imagined; I'm a little obsessive about that. Only sometimes have we had to renounce an idea because the materials simply can't do what I want them to do. Usually the artisans I collaborate with have never worked with materials the way they do on my pieces, even though they are experts, with decades of experience. That is why they often like to work with me, because they get to reinvent a technique and see how to make it possible. Mind you, sometimes they are not so happy to have to change everything they already know! For example, I have used Plexiglas in many projects for which I wanted it to be sculpted in a way they had never done before, as if the Plexiglas were a piece of marble or wood. They were all rather dubious.

AD: So do you think you're designing just to be provocative? To make things difficult?

MB: Life would be much simpler for everybody if I didn't keep coming up with these ideas, but I hate life to be simple! Yes, sometimes form follows function. . .but I don't want what function dictates. If you look at the Strata cabinet, at first it seems as if the metal were floating. You experience it visually first, but then you also have to experience it physically. The handles are not indicated so you don't know how or where to open it. That is done on purpose.

AD: And it would be terrible if you were desperate for a drink! So do you work in such a way that you come up with something entirely from imagination, and then try to turn it into a physical object?

MB: I try to situate myself and my designs into a gap where things do not exist. And it is this gap I always want to find, to explore all by myself, something in-between. I don't know if you can call my work only "design," or only "art"; it is something in-between, where there is a special space.

AD: Or as in Latin, *a tertium quid*—a "third thing." Surrealists created art that was also furniture, such as the Armoire Surréaliste, made by Marcel Jean in 1941, his Arbre Á tiroirs (Tree with Drawers) from 1942, Victor Brauner's Loup-table (Wolf-Table) from 1939 to 1947, and the Venus de Milo with Drawers (1936) and Mae West Lips sofa (1937) by Salvador Dalí.

MB: Dalí's idea was not primarily to make furniture, but to make sculpture. Somebody else came up with the plan of turning it into actual furniture. I see myself more as a furniture designer than purely an artist.

AD: There is a delicious quote by Raúl Ruiz: "The only thing I cannot stand is authenticity."

MB: I agree with that! I was brought up by parents who, just by their nature as antiques dealers, were obsessed with "authenticity" and with the "genuine," whereas I am totally free about such things. Because I don't actually know what "authenticity" is, my work poses the questions: What is authenticity? Is there only one kind?

AD: And so one doesn't know where "good taste" lies?

MB: No, but by contrast one thing that does exist is official taste, the doxa. And I'm afraid that reigns in every milieu, in everything, in art and in design. Most designers take my work as a joke; they would never consider it seriously. But because my work is truly Pop, meaning "popular," it fills a gap that is in the imagination of real people.

AD: Your attitude reminds me of the extreme kitsch of Jeff Koons's early work, which introduced, into a space reserved for a very small and very wealthy cultural elite, something that had not been allowed to be there.

MB: There is a definite connection between our work. I feel quite close to what he does, and what I also appreciate about it is the execution, which is impeccable. That is partly why I show in art galleries. It helps refine my work—and it doesn't hurt its sales. Unfortunately, if you really want to improve the quality of the fabrication of a piece, it will cost a fortune. One of my best collectors in New York is also a major Koons collector, so I eventually got in touch with a gentleman in Germany who makes some of Koons's pieces. He would have loved to fabricate my work for me, but it was just too expensive, as in ten times my normal budget.

AD: We're a long way from Renzo Mongiardino's style of turning "poor" materials to rich effect.

MB: But I'm also attracted to rich things that are rich! If I had to start now as a young designer, it would be very difficult—almost impossible—to work with no money. This was not the case when I began. For example, we only used wrought iron in the beginning because we didn't have enough money to cast bronze. But now it's not the materials that cost, it's the time and the labor. There will always be people making things themselves, with their own hands, but this investment is becoming increasingly expensive. Yet it is necessary that the quality of our workmanship is expensive.

AD: In your recent shows, the works are so different from each other that it's unclear when they were made, or even what era they are from.

MB: Or even if they were made by the same person! I show different things together: organic, Rococo forms, almost Bauhaus modernism. That's how I like to function now. I hate the idea of a "collection," where every piece has a prescribed relationship to each other. That's not how life is.

AD: Your work is very much about pushing the boundaries.

MB: As Gloria Swanson says in *Sunset Boulevard*, "It's the pictures that got small," which is exactly what has happened today. I'm interested in the idea of extreme glamour, but with quality. What I hate is the tyranny of the ordinary and the average. I detest Ikea.

AD: You are "IDEA" as opposed to "IKEA." It could be your logo.

MB: I could never stay alive by repeating the same thing again and again. I have an absolute fear of boredom.

AD: Is so-called art being taken more seriously than functional furniture?

MB: I don't really care if my pieces will be used or become objets d'art. But they are always functional. I worry about their functionality but I don't want my effort to be too obvious—a piece doesn't have to look as though it works. I like the idea of uncertainty, of people being disoriented. There is something about being uncertain about everything: the purpose of the object, what it is made of, the shapes, even whether it is beautiful or ugly, or heavy or light. I don't like certitude, the feeling that things are fixed once and for all. I like objects that can lose their balance, quite literally, and also make you lose your balance, mentally. I like very much when people don't know if they're on solid ground or very slippery territory.

AD: You have absolutely no fear of ever pushing it too far. . . . ?

MB: What is "too far"? I don't think I know what "too far" or "too much" ever can be!

MATTIA BONETTI'S STUDIO FAÇADE
Reduced-scale models of Mattia Bonetti designs

MATTIA BONETTI'S STUDIO
Reduced-scale models and 1:1 scale models
of Mattia Bonetti designs and jewelry

13

ABYSS DINING TABLE
Bronze with gold and silver plating
75 x 250 x 130 cm
29½ x 98⅜ x 51⅛ in
David Gill Galleries Edition
London, 2004

14

CHINA STANDARD LAMP
Glazed porcelain with platinum
details, gilded iron, silk shade
187 x 50 x 50 cm
73⅜ x 19¾ x 19¾ in
David Gill Galleries Edition
London, 2004

opposite page:

GEORGE SIDE TABLE/LAMP
Patinated bronze and blown glass
149 x 62.5 x 35 cm
58¾ x 24½ x 13⅞ in
Paul Kasmin Gallery Edition
New York, 2009

SALOME BG DINING TABLE
Large version with scagliola top
and patinated bronze columns
73 x 210 x 120 cm
28¾ x 82⅝ x 47¼ in
David Gill Galleries Edition
London, 1999

BOYS & GIRLS BG CANDLESTICKS
Patinated bronze,
Yellow and white gold leaf
35 x 25 x 25 cm
13¾ x 9⅞ x 9⅞ in
1994

INSPIRALE ESPIRALE BG ANDIRONS
Bronze
32 x 8 x 53 cm
12⅝ x 3⅛ x 20⅞ in
1989

DAY AND NIGHT STANDARD LAMP/MIRROR
Gold- and black nickel-plated brass, mirror, acrylic
204.5 x 80 x 35 cm
80½ x 31½ x 13¾ in
Paul Kasmin Gallery Edition
New York, 2009

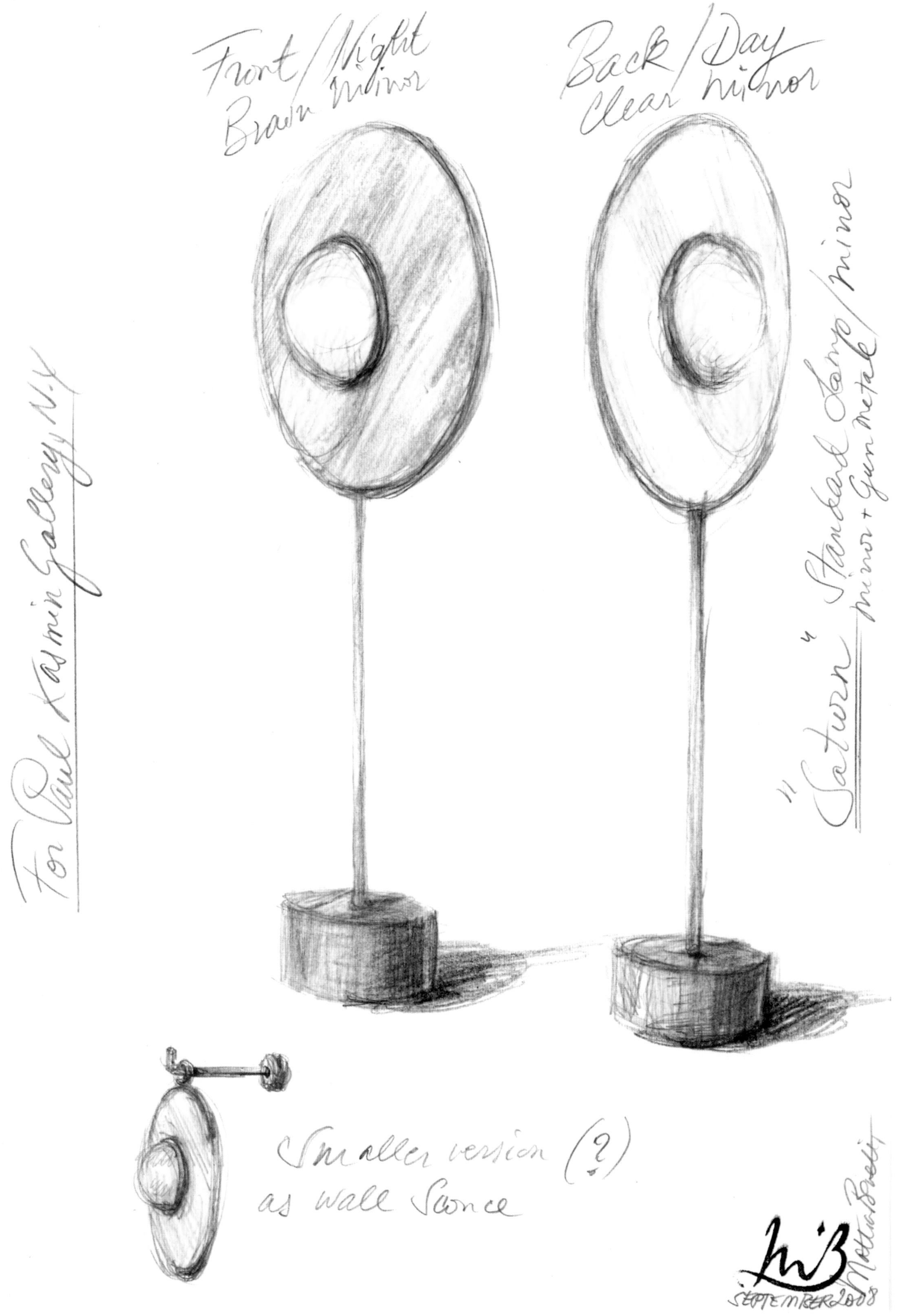
Front / Night
Brass mirror
Back / Day
Clear mirror
For Paul Kasmin Gallery, N.Y
"Saturn" Standard Lamp / mirror
mirror + Gun metal
Smaller version (?)
as wall Sconce
Mattia Bonetti
SEPTEMBER 2008

PRESS SOFA
Trompe-l'oeil painted wood structure
and embroidered upholstery
77 x 184 x 92 cm
30¼ x 72½ x 36¼ in
Contrast Gallery Edition
Shanghai, 2004

David Toppani sculptor

"With his help on prototypes and resin pieces, we push studies of shapes well beyond their boundaries." M.B.

Two-colours Gilded Resin Coffee-Table

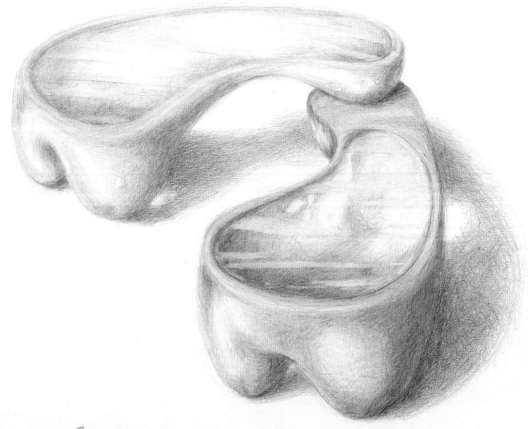

Mr. Jay Goldman, Drawing Room, New-York

September 2006

MR. JEAN-PIERRE WERTHEIM RESIDENCE

Desk: Patinated resin and wood
75 x 175 x 90 cm
29½ x 68⅞ x 35⅛ in
Paris, 2003

BG desk lamp
Patinated bronze
1992

BG standard lamp
White gold leaf gilded bronze
and silk lampshade with appliqué
2000

3 CIRCLES COFFEE TABLE
Lacquered fiberglass and glass
45 x 122 x 135 cm
17¼ x 48 x 53⅛ in
Édition La Galerie Italienne
Paris, 2008

opposite page:

CAILLOUX SOFA
Lacquered fiberglass with upholstery
95 x 224 x 112 cm
37⅛ x 88¼ x 44⅛ in
Édition La Galerie Italienne
Paris, 2007

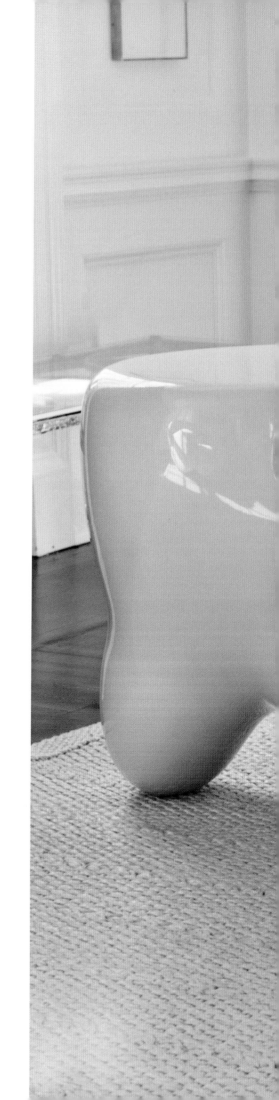

MR. JEAN-PIERRE LEHMANN AND MRS. RACHEL LEHMANN RESIDENCE

Side table: lacquered resin
Coffee table: mirror-polished stainless steel
Sofa: lacquered wood structure with upholstery
East Hampton, New York, 2004

PEARL COFFEE TABLE
Lacquered fiberglass
45 x 150 x 100 cm
17¾ x 59 x 39¾ in
David Gill Galleries Edition
London, 2008

When I first saw Mattia Bonetti's work at the Paris showroom of Christian Lacroix, his furniture struck me as so fresh and extravagant that I just had to have it for the drawing room of our castle in Regensburg. When my late husband wondered how to celebrate the five-hundredth anniversary of our postal service, which was also a jubilee for our family as we had invented it, I brought up the idea that Mattia and his then-partner might design a special entrance and café for the tourists who visit our castle. I thought there could be no better way to promote the modernity of our family nested in the ancient walls of St. Emmeram Castle. The castle had been a Benedictine monastery before the time of Napoleon's secularization policy, during which all church properties had been nationalized. Likewise, the king of Bavaria nationalized the postal service, and in return gave Thurn und Taxis the St. Emmeram properties in 1812. Mattia transformed the lobby and the café of our museum. The lamps that were designed looked like giant pink condoms, and all of my friends made fun of me! The chairs were green, made out of metal and upholstered with a bright pink material. It looked funky and new and I loved it. And to this day the café is a popular place for our visitors to sit and relax before visiting the huge *schloss.* My private drawing room that he designed is also still wonderful, proving that his work is truly timeless. The carpet and the sofas are violet velvet, with huge yellow sunflowers that had been sewn on by the very same craftsmen who do all the embroidery for Chanel. Now that I have a fresco by the German painter Andreas Schulze in the space, I know for a fact what I had always felt intuitively: This furniture looks even more elegant with contemporary art. Back then, when I originally commissioned these pieces, "art" was not to be combined with "applied art," as the taste then was more austere and reduced. But I did not like that. I always wanted contemporary design to live alongside contemporary art. And I am so happy that this has become quite normal today.

I wish Mattia Bonetti all the very best and huge success for the future. He has enlightened my life with his positivity and positively fun furniture and happy colors.

Princess Gloria von Thurn und Taxis

MATTIA BONETTI'S STUDIO

CHEWING GUM SIDE TABLE
Aluminum, metallic paint, glass top
65 x 71 x 43 cm
25⅛ x 28 x 16⅞ in
David Gill Galleries Edition
London, 2008

Structure en Chêne sablé et doré de couleurs, Literie et

jeté de Lit en Lin avec applications

en Cuir métallisé

AVRIL 2008

TUTTI FRUTTI TABLE
Color gilded oak and clear acrylic top
75 x 130 x 130 cm
29½ x 51 x 51 in
Édition Galerie Cat-Berro
Paris, 2008

opposite page:

HAPPY BIRTHDAY CABINET
Cast bronze, gilded varnish,
aluminum leaf, wood
120 x 120 x 60 cm
47¼ x 47¼ x 23⅜ in
David Gill Galleries Edition
London, 2008

MR. GEORGE LINDEMANN, JR.
AND MR. ESTEBAN LONDONO RESIDENCE

LXVI chairs: hand-sculpted wood, white, yellow,
and color gilding, Aubusson tapestry
Miami Beach, 2004/2005

ABYSS DINING TABLE
(See pages 14-15)

42

TOAST SIDE TABLE
Lacquered fiberglass
60 x 67 x 57 cm
23⅝ x 26⅛ x 22½ in
David Gill Galleries Edition
London, 2008

opposite page:

HEATHER CHEST OF DRAWERS
Lacquered fiberglass and stained mahogany
99 x 130 x 65 cm
39 x 51⅛ x 25⅝ in
David Gill Galleries Edition
London, 2008

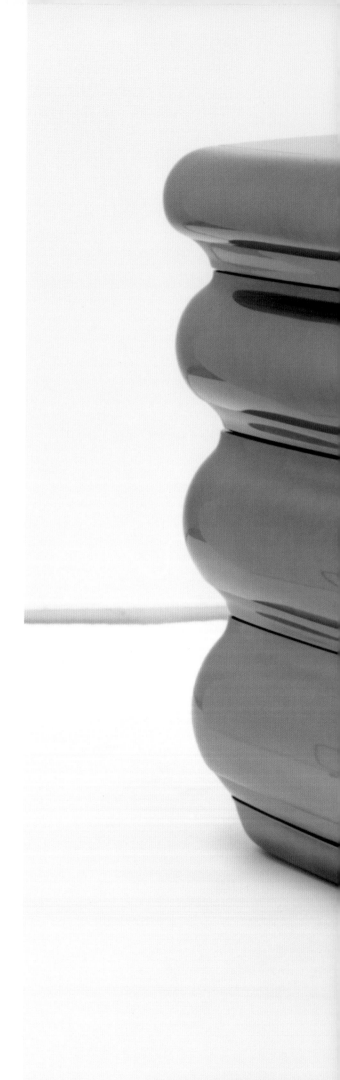

for the PAUL KASMIN GALLERY, New York

"Ever"

Chair

Cast & Gilded bronze structure

"Ever"

Low Armchair

Cast & patinated bronze structure &
an upholstered seat

MARCH 2008

Jocelyne Emerit gilder

"She has been my gilder for over twenty years. Her talent has made our color gilding possible." M.B.

MRS. JOCELYNE EMERIT'S STUDIO
Mattia Bonetti standard lamp:
partially gilded wrought-iron, parchment

following page:

Gilded wrought-iron headboard

FREQUENCY CABINET
Clear acrylic and gold-plated brass
200.5 x 90 x 53.5 cm
79 x 35½ x 21 in
Paul Kasmin Gallery Edition, prototype
New York, 2009

opposite page:

MATTIA BONETTI'S STUDIO
1:1 scale models for Metz Cathedral designs

THE METZ CATHEDRAL

ST. ÉTIÈNNE DE METZ
CATHEDRAL CHOIR
Chairs: oak and horse hair fabric
Candlestick: partially gilded bronze
Cross: gilded bronze

opposite page:

Altar: partially gilded bronze, marble,
Beauvais-manufacture tapestry

57

MR. PIERRE BASSE'S STUDIO
Armchair (work in progress)
Wrought-iron

efore meeting Mattia in his studio, I had anticipated seeing the eccentric, chaotic environment of a modern-day mad scientist. I was struck by the utter simplicity of his workplace, which is in marked contrast to the wild complexity of his creative output. Likewise, his demeanor, reserved and thoughtful, belies the fantastical machine that resides deep within his brilliant and creative mind.

Mattia is unencumbered by history; the traditions of form, functionality, and materials gracefully acquiesce to his vision. His mastery of technique is never an end in itself but a point of departure—something I witnessed when I visited the craftspeople he engages, as they are constantly challenged to reimagine or subvert their knowledge of their applied arts.

As a designer, I am humbled by his boundless imagination and his eternal quest for "the new." The process of creating this book has enhanced my admiration of Mattia's work and given me a deeper, albeit fleeting, view into his wonderland.

Reed Krakoff

Pierre Basse art blacksmith

"A partner of mine since my very early days, before that he was Diego Giacometti's blacksmith.

His talent enables me to bend metal to follow my desires." M.B.

MR. PIERRE BASSE'S STUDIO

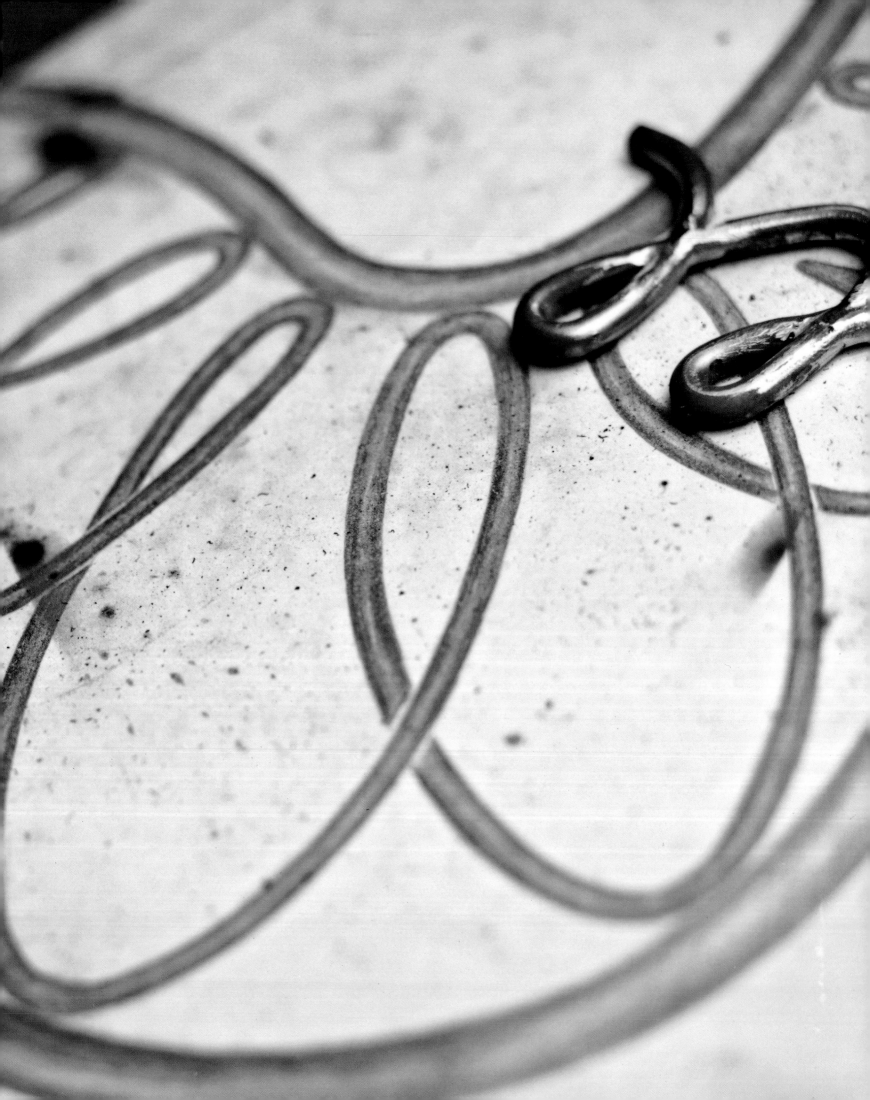

"Meander" Coffee Table, Cast Bronze Base & Acrylic Top
For the PAUL KASMIN GALLERY, New York
NOVEMBER 2008

Mattia Bonetti

QUASIMODO CABINET
Patinated resin, tinted wood,
patinated wrought-iron
204.5 x 89 x 71 cm
80½ x 35 x 28 in
Paul Kasmin Gallery Edition
New York, 2009

opposite page:
MATTIA BONETTI'S STUDIO
Reduced-scale models of
Mattia Bonetti designs, books
and objects

DELPHINE AND REED KRAKOFF RESIDENCE

MEANDER COFFEE TABLE
Patinated bronze and clear acrylic top
58.5 x 145 x 145 cm
23 x 57 x 57 in
Paul Kasmin Gallery Edition
New York, 2009

ALU CHAIR
(See page 79)

GEORGE SIDE TABLE/LAMP
(See page 17)

Laurent Roca art woodworker

"His mastery of wood sculpture can transform my seats into realities." M.B.

MR. LAURENT ROCA'S STUDIO

UFO SIDE TABLE
Tinted oak and cast bronze
65 x 50 x 50 cm
25⅝ x 19¼ x 19¼ in
Édition Galerie Cat-Berro
Paris, 2008

Galerie Catberro Paris
"Vagues"
Buffet à trois portes en chêne et bronze poli

AVRIL 2008

ONDE TABLE
Solid oak and polished brass
75 x 180 x 88 cm
29½ x 70⅞ x 34⅝ in
Édition Galerie Cat-Berro
Paris, 2006

WALL CHEST
Scarified oak and elm
100 x 120 x 50 cm
39⅛ x 47¼ x 19¾ in
Édition Galerie Cat-Berro
Paris, 2007

opposite page:

ALU CHAIR
Lacquered aluminum,
upholstery with appliqué
110 x 46.5 x 59 cm
43¼ x 18¼ x 23¼ in
Paul Kasmin Gallery Edition
New York, 2009

MR. JEAN-PIERRE LEHMANN AND MRS. RACHEL LEHMANN RESIDENCE

Armchairs: patinated wood structure,
painted and polished brass, upholstery
Coffee table: gilded hand-sculpted wood
and clear acrylic top
East Hampton, New York, 2004

"Drawing Room"
Mr. Jay Goldman, Long Island
Cast & Patinated Bronze Double Table

DECEMBER 2005

Chêne Valdé Xtra-Sablé
+ métallisation gris foncé
manchettes cuir noir

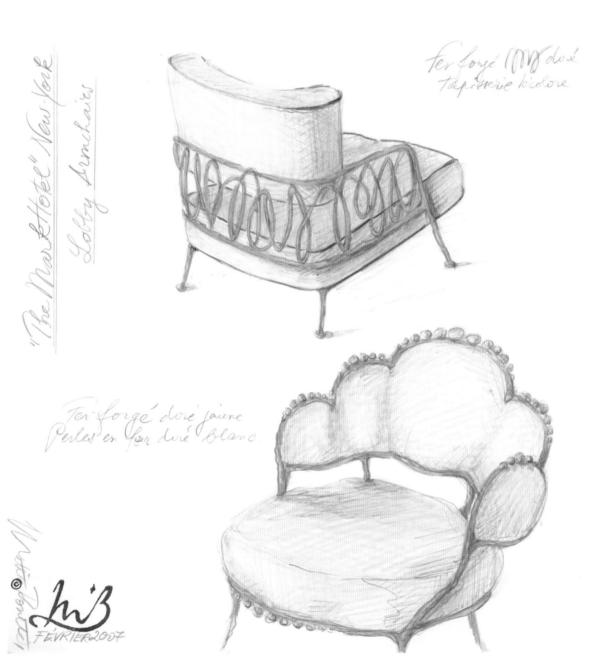

fer forgé MMS doré
tapisserie bicolore

"The MarkHôtel" New-York
Lobby Armchairs

Fer forgé doré jaune
Perles en fer doré blanc

FÉVRIER 2007

attia Bonetti is an enigma. Debates about him have raged since 1992 when, at the request of the president of the Centre Pompidou, I started the National Museum of Modern Art's design collection. Is he a designer? A decorator? A sculptor? An interior architect? Does he even belong in the Centre Pompidou's collection? Can the design world include this artist, whose work defies the simple classification necessary for protection from critics and analyzing curators' positions, which are always subjective? This debate is because design, since Bauhaus and the Ulm School, has returned the value of an object to its function, as in the now famous saying "form follows function," suppressing useless and frivolous decor. Beyond the debates, Bonetti's work has a strong presence in the collection, from individual pieces—provocative and unique furniture—to a series of makeup packaging conceived for Nina Ricci.

The French and Europeans love to classify according to so-called rational criteria, yet Mattia Bonetti is unclassifiable. Bonetti's strength is in transgressing codes, eras; in daring to use humor, color, a childlike spirit, the pleasure of decor; in using diverse influences, from woodworkers of the eighteenth century to those of the Art Deco movement; in portraying himself with absolute command of execution and craftsmanship during an era prone to minimalism and atonal color. I believe that the design collection at the museum should be enriched with the inclusion of more surrealist furniture like the Happy Birthday cabinet. I am amused, sometimes annoyed, yet always interested by the freedom of Mattia Bonetti, who conceived the layout of the choir of the Metz Cathedral after having decorated the Montpellier tramway, while also creating fantastical furniture influenced by an imagined history. Who is he? Where is he? In his bare and maniacally ordered studio, Bonetti can give himself entirely to his imagination. But he's not a poet or a utopian—his objects and furniture actually work! I mean to say, by reflecting emotions, he surprises and amuses us and questions our "good taste," so petit-bourgeois, so mainstream! If I were to steal an object of Mattia's, it would be the Abyss table from 2004. His singular trajectory, of which the media is so unaware, merits being part of a public collection that is witness to the profusion of contemporary creativity.

Marie-Laure Jousset

MR. GEORGE LINDEMANN, JR.
AND MR. ESTEBAN LONDONO RESIDENCE

Armchair: gilded wrought-iron, wood structure
and leather upholstery
Sofa: wood structure with upholstery
Miami Beach, 2004/2005

CUT OUT SOFA
Wood structure with leather upholstery
91 x 136 x 79 cm
35⅛ x 53½ x 31⅛ in
David Gill Galleries Edition
London, 2004

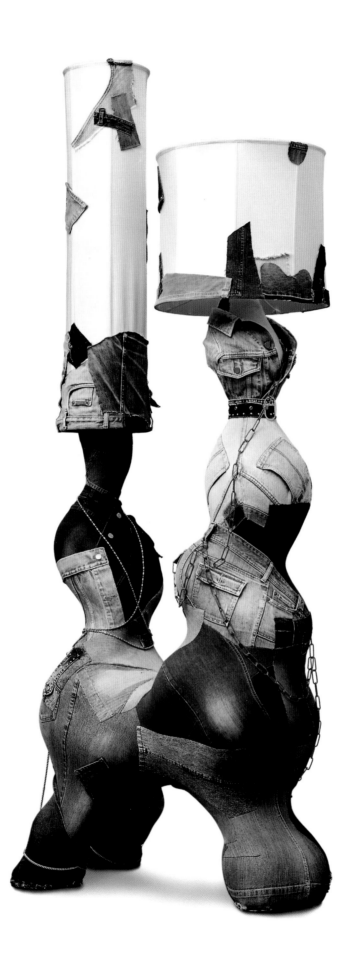

DENIM STANDARD LAMP
Resin base with denim upholstery,
metal accessories, silk and
denim lampshades
220.5 x 85 x 49.5 cm
86¼ x 33½ x 19½ in
Édition La Galerie Italienne
Paris, 2007

opposite page:

DENIM ARMCHAIR
Denim upholstery, metal and
leather accessories
99 x 100.5 x 96.5 cm
39 x 39½ x 38 in
Édition La Galerie Italienne
Paris, 2007

POLYHEDRAL CHEST OF DRAWERS
Polished stainless steel and ebonized mahogany
102 x 150 x 75 cm
40⅛ x 59 x 29½ in
David Gill Galleries Edition
London, 2004

opposite page:

MR. DAVID GILL AND
MR. FRANCIS SULTANA RESIDENCE

ALU CONSOLE
Embossed aluminum
100 x 169 x 40 cm
39⅛ x 66½ x 15¼ in
David Gill Galleries Edition
London, 2008

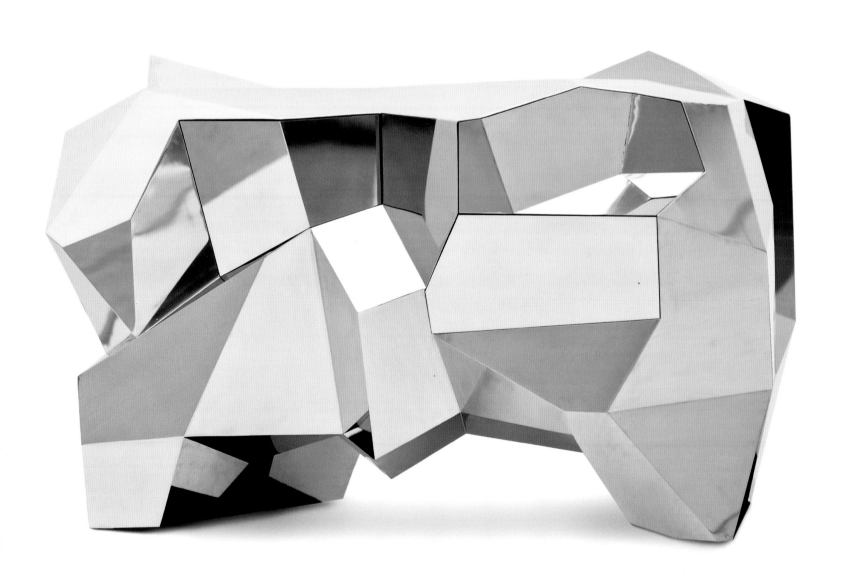

BRANCHES WALL/CEILING LAMPS/MIRRORS
Yellow, white and moongold gilded or
lacquered resin, mirror or frosted glass
Paul Kasmin Gallery Edition
New York, 2009

1 BRANCH
37 x 31 x 39.5 cm
14½ x 12⅛ x 15½ in

3 BRANCHES
55 x 74.5 x 46.5 cm
21½ x 29¼ x 18⅛ in

5 BRANCHES
84 x 89 x 57 cm
33 x 35 x 22⅜ in

SPHERE STANDARD LAMP
Chromium-plated steel and glass
200 x 50 x 55 cm
78¾ x 19¼ x 21⅛ in
David Gill Galleries Edition
London, 2008

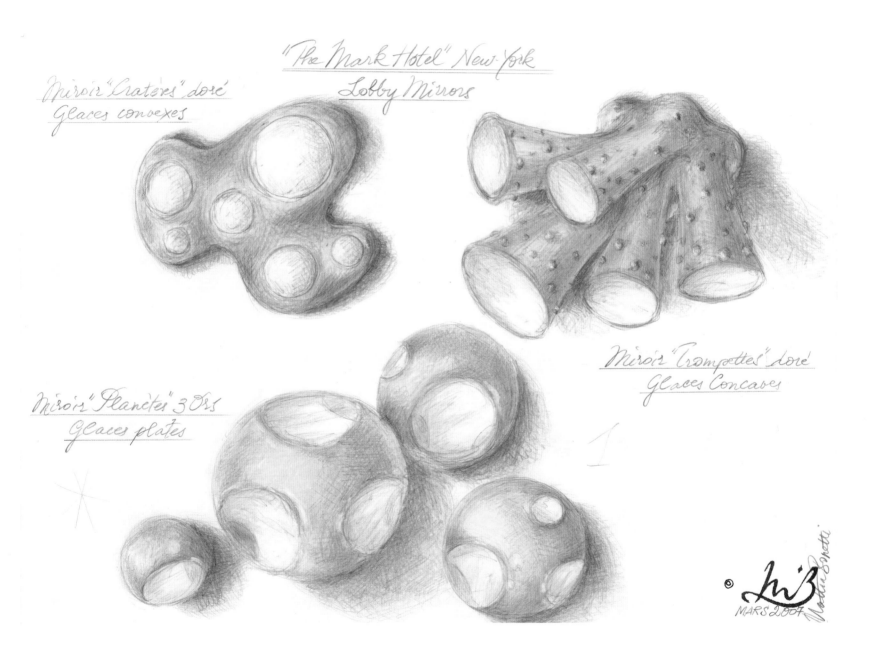

Miroir "Cratères" doré
Glaces convexes

"The Mark Hotel" New-York
Lobby Mirrors

Miroir "Trompettes" doré
Glaces Concaves

Miroir "Planètes" 3 Ors
Glaces plates

MARS 2007

97

YO-YO TABLE
Embossed aluminum
43 x 140 x 140 cm
16⅞ x 55⅛ x 55⅛ in
David Gill Galleries Edition
London, 2008

opposite page:

BUBBLES CHEST
Natural steel
122 x 158 x 55 cm
48 x 62¼ x 21⅛ in
Édition La Galerie Italienne
Paris, 2007

BLOB MIRROR
Mirror and sculpted alder wood
70 x 70 cm
27½ x 27½ in

Édition Galerie Cat-Berro
Paris, 2008

have much admiration for Mattia Bonetti, so talking about him is a pleasure. We have known each other for many years and I have always followed his work with great interest.

Bonetti's talent is unique among designers. Every time he has created pieces for my projects, I have never been disappointed. Astonishing ideas flow out of him in diverse and unpredictable ways, their paths sometimes converging, sometimes diverging, but always endlessly inventive. His artistic vision challenges us, yet it is also responsive to what gives us pleasure. Matching the buoyancy of his fantastical designs is the lightness with which he speaks about his work.

In all of these ways and more, he is an inspiration to me.

Jacques Grange

NECKLACE CONSOLE TABLE
Polished stainless steel
and black nickel-plated brass
91 x 129 x 30 cm
35¼ x 50¾ x 11¼ in
Paul Kasmin Gallery Edition
New York, 2009

opposite page:

NECKLACE SIDE TABLE
Polished stainless steel
and black nickel-plated brass
58 x 74 x 54.5 cm
22¼ x 29⅛ x 21⅛ in
Paul Kasmin Gallery Edition
New York, 2009

CITY LAMP
Nickel- and gold-plated steel,
lacquered wood, and glass
74 x 41.5 x 36.5 cm
29½ x 16⅛ x 14⅛ in
David Gill Galleries Edition
London, 2004

opposite page:

CARDS COMMODE
Polished stainless steel,
colored acrylic, wood
122 x 168 x 78 cm
48 x 66 x 30 in
Paul Kasmin Gallery Edition, prototype
New York, 2009

STRATA CABINET
Polished stainless steel
170 x 81 x 48 cm
66⅛ x 32⅛ x 18⅞ in
David Gill Galleries Edition
London, 2004

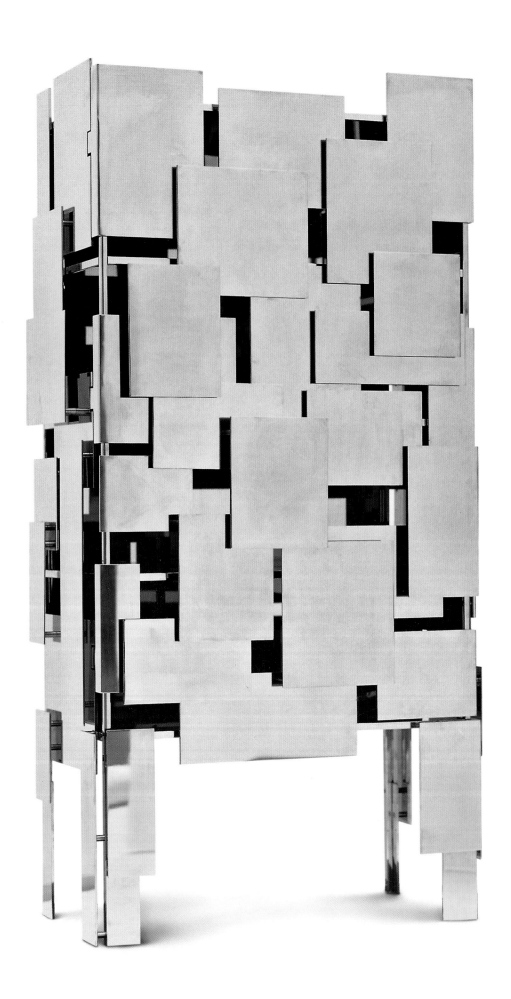

Mr. and Mrs. Jean-Pierre Lehmann, East Hampton - USA
Polished and Waxed Steel "Polyhedral" Coffee-Tables
AUGUST 2007   Mattia Bonetti

VORTEX DINING TABLE
Aluminum and clear acrylic
75 x 130 x 130 cm
29½ x 51⅛ x 51⅛ in
Paul Kasmin Gallery Edition
New York, 2009

JEWELRY
Mediterranean pebbles, pearls, diamonds, gold, silver

PUBLISHED BY SKIRA RIZZOLI IN ASSOCIATION WITH
PAUL KASMIN GALLERY AND REED KRAKOFF ON THE OCCASION OF THE EXHIBITION:

MATTIA BONETTI

PAUL KASMIN GALLERY

FEBRUARY 11 – MARCH 13, 2010

293 TENTH AVENUE

NEW YORK, NY 10001

DEDICATIONS

I am profoundly indebted to my parents, Giorgio and Stella Bonetti, who recognized my artistic sensitivity in childhood and nurtured it throughout my life. To my wife, Isabelle, and my daughters, Louise and Laure, for their patience and affection.

To Régis de Saintdo, who has assisted me for many years with inspiring intelligence and fidelity. To my successive gallerists—Pierre Staudenmeyer and Gérard Dalmon; David Gill and Françis Sultana; Francis Cat-Berro and Véronique Sainten; Xavier Hufkens and Pierre-Marie Giraud; and Alessandro and Anna Pron—who have all both given my work exposure and sold it with audacity and enthusiasm.

To Paul Kasmin and Reed Krakoff, who originated this book. To David Whitney, who was and remains my guardian angel. To my friends Yves Oppenheim, Samia Saouma-Hetzler, Peter Dunham and Madison Cox for their friendship and their counsel. And to all who gave me their support.

— Mattia Bonetti

To my wife, Delphine, who, like Mattia's creations, exudes beauty, intelligence, strength, humor, and—most of all—magic.

I want to thank Mattia for his kindness and generosity for letting me into his gorgeous, fascinating, and brilliant world.

I also want to express my gratitude to the following people: Cari Vuong, Rebecca Wong Young, Raina Penchansky, Heather Feit, Régis de Saintdo, Paul Kasmin, Nicholas Olney, Anne Halber-Dessaint, Charles Miers, and Dung Ngo.

— Reed Krakoff

ACKNOWLEDGMENTS

The publishers would like to thank:

Mattia Bonetti for the privilege of creating this book, Régis de Saintdo for his invaluable assistance, and the gifted artisans for sharing their studios and craftsmanship.

David Gill and Francis Sultana from David Gill Galleries in London, Francis Cat-Berro and Véronique Sainten from the Cat-Berro Gallery in Paris, Alessandro and Anna Pron from the Galerie Italienne in Paris, and Nicholas Olney and Paul Kasmin from the Paul Kasmin Gallery in New York for their extraordinary effort and expertise.

Adrian Dannatt for his elegant foreword, and Princess Gloria von Thurn und Taxis, Reed Krakoff, Marie-Laure Jousset, and Jacques Grange for their insightful essays.

Chanoine Gabriel Normand and the Chapitre de la Cathédrale de Metz, for their gracious welcome to the Saint Étienne Cathedral in Metz, Jean-Pierre and Rachel Lehmann in East Hampton, New York; George Lindeman, Jr. and Esteban Londono in Miami, Florida; and Jean-Pierre Wertheim in Paris for their generous hospitality.

EXHIBITIONS

INDIVIDUAL EXHIBITIONS
Néotu Gallery, Paris

En attendant les Barbares, Paris

David Gill Gallery, London

Kulturring Stadtgalerie, Sundern, Germany

The Hydra Workshop Foundation,
Hydra, Greece

Musée F. Mandet, Riom, France

Le Centre Georges Pompidou, Paris

Seibu Museum, Tokyo

Le Grand Hornu, Hornu, Belgium

Luhring Augustine, New York

Galerie Cat-Berro, Paris

Galerie Xavier Hufkens, Brussels, Belgium

Galerie Italienne, Paris

Paul Kasmin Gallery, New York

GROUP EXHIBITIONS
Victoria and Albert Museum, London

Kunstmuseum, Düsseldorf, Germany

Musée des Arts Décoratifs, Paris

Design Museum, Frankfurt am Main, Germany

Cooper-Hewitt Museum, New York

Tel Aviv Museum, Israel

Guggenheim Museum, New York

Le Centre Georges Pompidou, Paris

PUBLIC COLLECTIONS

Le Centre Georges Pompidou, Paris

Musée des Arts Décoratifs, Paris

Musée F. Mandet, Riom-France

Seibu Museum, Tokyo

Le Grand Hornu, Hornu, Belgium

Design Museum, Frankfurt am Main, Germany

Kunstmuseum, Düsseldorf, Germany

Cooper-Hewitt Museum, New York

Victoria and Albert Museum, London

CREDITS

Saint Étienne Cathedral in Metz, France:
Furniture: property of the Fabrique de la
Cathédral. Tapestry: woven by the National
Manufactory of Beauvais and property of the
State (Mobilier National). These works were
realized with the participation of the Direction
Régionale of the cultural affairs of Lorraine
and the Arts Plastiques delegation of the
French ministry of culture and communication.

Photography: Reed Krakoff
(except as noted below)
Cari Vuong: pages 2-3, 17, 18-19, 20, 30, 31,
34, 37, 40, 41, 44, 45, 53, 66, 74, 78, 90, 91,
92, 93, 94, 95, 96, 98, 99, 102, 103, 104-105,
106, 108-109
Sasha Gusov, courtesy of David Gill Galleries:
pages 88-89, 105
Stéphane Briolant, courtesy of
Galerie Cat-Berro: 76-77, 100
Courtesy of David Gill Galleries: pages 14-15

Editor: Dung Ngo
Creative Direction: Rebecca Wong Young
Design: Alberta Testanero
Production: Maria Pia Gramaglia,
James Stathatos, Kevin Canfield
Project Coordinator: Anne Halber-Dessaint

BIBLIOGRAPHY

French/English monograph, published by
Michel Aveline, Paris, 1990

German/English monograph, published
by Form Verlag-Frankfurt am Main, West
Germany, 1966

French/English monograph, published by
Dis-Voir, Paris, 1998

French/English monograph, published by
La Lettre Volée, Brussels, 2001

English monograph, Mattia Bonetti
Drawings, introduction by Carol Vogel,
published by Calluna Farms Press and
Luhring Augustine, New York, 2005

First published in the United States of America in 2010 by
RIZZOLI INTERNATIONAL PUBLICATIONS, INC.
300 Park Avenue South
New York, NY 10010
www.rizzoliusa.com

PAUL KASMIN GALLERY
293 Tenth Avenue
New York, NY 10001
www.paulkasmingallery.com

ISBN-13: 978-0-8478-3417-4
Library of Congress Control Number: 2009929563

Distributed to the U.S. trade by Random House, New York

Printed and bound in China

2010 2011 2012 2013 2014 / 10 9 8 7 6 5 4 3 2 1